Crabapples

BEARS

Bobbie Kalman & Tammy Everts

Crabtree Publishing Company

Crabapples

created by bobbie kalman

for Merle Elder, who inspired the Crabapples

Editor-in-Chief
Bobbie Kalman

Writing team
Bobbie Kalman
Tammy Everts

Managing editor
Lynda Hale

Editors
Petrina Gentile
Janine Schaub

Computer design
Lynda Hale
David Schimpky

Color separations and film
Dot 'n Line Image Inc.

Printer
Worzalla Publishing Company

Illustrations
Barb Bedell: pages 6, 16-17
Tammy Everts: page 11
Barb Hinterhoeller: page 13
Ellen O'Hara: pages 8, 14-15, 18

Photographs
All photographs were provided by Tom Stack & Associates.
They were taken by the following photographers:
Nancy Adams: page 29
W. Perry Conway: page 18
Susan Gibler: page 14
Victoria Hurst: front cover, pages 6, 20
Thomas Kitchin: back cover, pages 7 (top right), 8-9, 22-23, 30
Bob McKeever: page 28
Gary Milburn: pages 8 (bottom), 26, 27
Mark Newman: pages 4 (top), 5, 7 (left), 12 (top), 25
Brian Parker: pages 10, 24
Wendy Shattil & Bob Rozinski: page 23 (bottom)
John Shaw: pages 4 (bottom), 7 (bottom), 11, 12 (bottom), 15, 21
Richard P. Smith: title page
Anna E. Zuckerman: page 19

Crabtree Publishing Company

350 Fifth Avenue	360 York Road, RR 4	73 Lime Walk
Suite 3308	Niagara-on-the-Lake	Headington
New York	Ontario, Canada	Oxford OX3 7AD
N.Y. 10118	L0S 1J0	United Kingdom

Cataloging in Publication Data
Kalman, Bobbie, 1947-
  Bears

(Crabapples)
Includes index.

ISBN 0-86505-612-9 (library bound)   ISBN 0-86505-712-5 (pbk.)
This book examines the features and behavior of various bear species.

1. Bears - Juvenile literature. I. Everts, Tammy, 1970-
II. Title. III. Series: Kalman, Bobbie, 1947-   . Crabapples.

QL737.C27K35 1994   j599.74'446   LC 94-27536
                                                 CIP

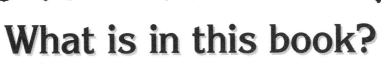

What is in this book?

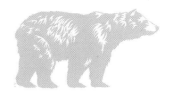

What are bears?

Bears are wild animals. They can be big or small. They can have black, white, red, gold, or brown fur. You can hug a teddy bear, but don't try to hug this bear!

Bears are **plantigrade** animals. People are plantigrade animals, too. Plantigrade animals walk flat on their feet instead of on their toes. Bears sometimes stand on their back legs. When they stand, they can see things that are far away.

Bears are **mammals**. Mammals have hair or fur. Female mammals carry their babies inside their body until the babies are born. The babies feed on their mother's milk.

Bear facts

Some people believe that bears cannot see well, but bears have very good vision.

All bears have small round ears. Their hearing is much better than ours.

Bears have five toes and five sharp claws on each foot. They have short tails.

Bears have both sharp teeth and flat teeth for biting and chewing their food.

A bear's long nose looks like that of a dog. Bears have an excellent sense of smell.

Bears have short legs. Short legs make them look slow and clumsy, but they can run much faster than people can.

Bears have different kinds of fur. Their fur suits the climate in which they live. Fur can keep a bear warm or cool. Polar bear fur is made up of both long and short hairs. The long hairs keep snow away from the bear's body. Under the long fur, short **guard hairs** trap the polar bear's body heat next to its skin.

Bears have enormous appetites. They spend most of their time looking for food. These brown bear cubs are ready to pounce on a delicious fish dinner.

Where do bears live?

Some bears live in mountain caves.
Some bears live in snowy burrows.
Some bears live in dens of earth.
Some bears live in leafy nests.
Bears can live almost anywhere!

What's for dinner?

Most bears are **omnivores**. Omnivores eat both plants and animals. People are also omnivores. Bears eat meat, plants, berries, insects, and honey. They even eat the bees that make the honey! Some bears catch fish in rivers and lakes. Some visit garbage dumps to find food. Most bears are not fussy eaters.

Sleeping bears

Bears that live in warm places stay awake during the winter. Bears that live in cold places sleep through the winter because there is not enough food to eat. This long sleep is called **hibernation**.

In autumn, a bear eats until it gets very fat. Then it curls up in a hole or cave and sleeps. When the bear wakes up in spring, it is thin, hungry, and grouchy!

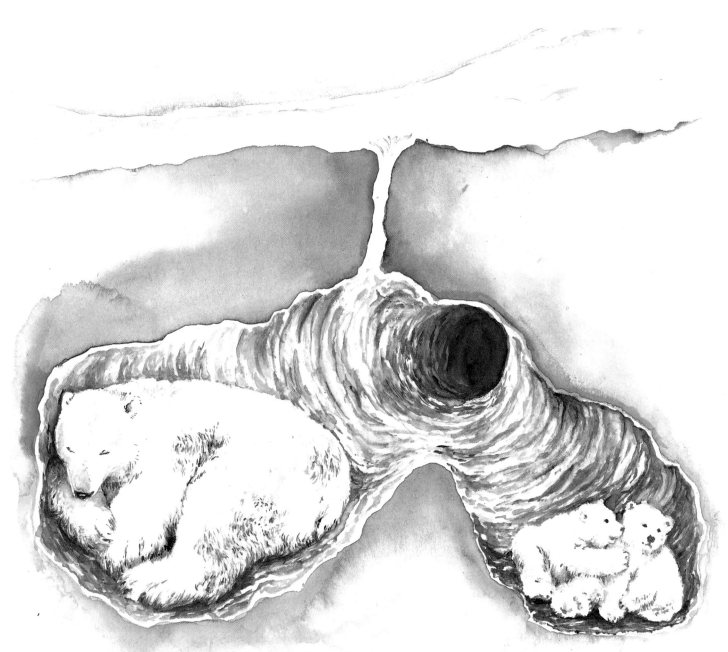

Female bears have babies during their
winter sleep! A polar bear mother
builds a den with two rooms before
winter sets in. She sleeps in one room.
Her cubs play in the other room.

Bouncing cubs

A mother bear can have one, two, three, or four babies. They are called **cubs**. Cubs are very small when they are born. They are blind and have no fur. Bear cubs stay with their mother for two years. The mother bear teaches them how to hunt and find food. The father bear leaves before the cubs are born.

Bear cubs love to play. They hug each
other. They wrestle. They explore. They
chase one another. Most bear cubs learn
to climb trees while they are very young
in case they need to escape from animals
that hunt them. Even male bears eat
newborn cubs.

The bear family tree

There are eight different species of bears, but some species have more than one kind of bear. The brown bear, for example, is one species of bear, but Kodiaks and grizzlies are both part of the brown bear family. The same is true of black bears. The Kermode is one kind of black bear.

The **miacid** lived 40 million years ago. It is the ancestor of dogs, bears, raccoons, and other mammals that eat meat.

dog

polar bear   brown bear   black bear   sun bear

The koala is not a bear!

Many people think koalas are bears, but they are not bears. The koala lives in Australia, and there are no real bears in Australia. A koala looks like a bear, but it is a **marsupial**. Female marsupials have a pouch on their stomach for carrying their baby.

The red panda is like a raccoon.

The giant panda is a bear.

raccoon

red panda

giant panda

Some scientists feel that pandas belong to their own family.

moon bear

sloth bear

spectacled bear

Polar bears

The polar bear is the largest of all bears. It lives in the far north, where there is lots of snow and ice. Its thick, white coat and furry foot pads keep the polar bear from feeling the cold. A layer of fat under its skin also keeps this big bear warm.

The long, wide feet of polar bears help them swim fast. On land, their big feet prevent them from sinking into the snow. Their foot pads stop them from slipping.

Polar bears eat seals, young walruses, and fish. They hunt on land and in the chilly arctic water. Mother bears teach their cubs how to catch seals.

Brown bears

There are many kinds of brown bears. The grizzly is one type. The Kodiak is the largest brown bear.

Brown bears are very smart. They can run fast, and they have strong teeth and powerful jaws.

Brown bears are not picky eaters. They eat almost anything, including plants, fish, eggs, and insects. They have long claws for digging mice out of the ground.

Black bears

Black bears are smaller than brown bears. They swim well, and they are good at catching fish with their paws.

Not all black bears have black fur. Some black bears are brown. Some are the color of cinnamon! The black bear in the picture below has golden fur. It is a Kermode. This rare bear is sometimes called a "ghost bear" because of its light color.

The sun bear

The sun bear is the smallest member of the bear family. It is only as big as a large dog. It has short, shiny black fur. The large yellow patch on its chest resembles the rising sun. That is how the sun bear got its name.

Although this bear is called a sun bear, it sleeps during the day! It often sleeps high up in a shady tree. At night, sun bears search for insects and fruit to eat. There is always plenty of food in their warm forest home, so sun bears do not need to hibernate.

The moon bear

The moon bear has silky, shaggy fur and a moon-shaped mark on its chest. That is why it is called a moon bear. The moon bear is also called the Asiatic black bear.

In summer, the moon bear lives in cool mountain areas. In winter, female moon bears hibernate and give birth to cubs.

Some male moon bears move down the mountains to warmer areas, where there are plenty of ants, nuts, and berries to eat.

The sloth bear

The sloth bear lives in hot rain forests, where there is plenty to eat all year long. It does not need to hibernate in the winter.

Sloth bears eat ants, termites, and bees. They use their long, curved claws to break open insect homes. They also use their claws to climb trees.

The sloth bear's claws are made of ivory. Which animal has tusks made of ivory? Did you guess the elephant? You were right!

The spectacled bear

"Spectacles" is an old name for eyeglasses. The spectacled bear has white markings around its eyes. Some people think these markings look like eyeglasses.

Spectacled bears live in hot, hilly areas, where there is always food. They do not need to hibernate.

Spectacled bears build nests in trees. They rest and eat in their nests. They eat mostly fruit, but sometimes they also hunt small animals.

Pandas

There are two types of pandas. One is the giant panda, and the other is the red panda. Both live in the mountains of China. Both eat bamboo leaves and shoots. They eat all year long. They do not hibernate.

The red panda is much smaller than the giant panda. It is sometimes called the **lesser panda**. Both red pandas and giant pandas are **rare**. When an animal is rare, it means that there are only a few of that kind of animal in the world.

People used to believe that both pandas were related to raccoons. Now we know that red pandas are more like raccoons, but giant pandas are definitely bears!

raccoon

Bears in danger

Bears are big animals. Big animals need big spaces to search for food. People have cut down trees and built houses in places where bears and other animals used to live. There are not many big, wild spaces left.

Some people are working hard to make sure that wild animals have places to live. They have set aside large parks where no one is allowed to build homes. These parks are called **national parks** or **reserves**.

Words to know

ancestor Something from which something or someone is descended
guard hairs The short fur close to a polar bear's skin
hibernate A long winter sleep
mammals Warm-blooded animals with backbones and hair or fur

marsupial An animal that carries its young in a pouch
omnivore An animal that feeds on both animals and plants
plantigrade Describing an animal that walks with the entire lower part of its foot on the ground

Index

What is in the picture?

Here is more information about the photographs in this book.

page:

front cover	A grizzly bear cub
back cover	North American black bear cubs
title page	A North American black bear mother with her cubs. Mother bears are very protective.
4 (top)	Brown bears live in Canada, Alaska, and parts of the United States.
4 (bottom)	A grizzly bear can be over 2.5 meters (8 feet) tall when it is standing!
5	This grizzly bear and her cub were photographed in Alaska.
6	Baby grizzlies often have a white band of fur around their neck.
7 (left)	Polar bears live in the far north of North America, Greenland, and Asia.
7 (top right)	This grizzly bear lives in the Rocky Mountains.
7 (bottom left)	These brown bear cubs are fishing for salmon in an Alaskan river.
8	This polar bear walks across the arctic snow. Polar bears cover hundreds of miles when hunting.
8-9	Hidden among tree branches, this bear cub is safe from enemies.
10	A North American black bear enjoys a meal of sweet wild berries.
11	This brown bear is fishing in a river in Katmai National Park, Alaska.
12 (top)	Polar bears have no enemies in the wild, so they can take a nap anywhere without worrying.
12 (bottom)	Three brown bears wait for salmon to leap up this waterfall.

page:

14	These brown bear cubs are growing quickly. Soon they will be as big as their mother.
15	All bear cubs are playful, but North American black bear cubs are especially active.
18	A polar bear swims in Wager Bay in Canada's Northwest Territories.
19	Polar bear cubs stay with their mother for two-and-a-half years.
20	A grizzly cub enjoys the spring after the long, cold winter.
21	Male grizzly bears roar at anything that enters their territory.
22-23	Like all babies, these black bear cubs need plenty of rest.
23	The Kermode's golden fur once made it a prize for hunters. Today it is illegal to hunt these bears.
24	The sun bear lives in parts of southern Asia.
25	The moon bear lives in Asia.
26	The sloth bear lives in parts of southern Asia.
27	The spectacled bear is the only bear that lives in South America.
28	Giant pandas must eat 18 kilograms (40 pounds) of bamboo shoots every day!
29	The red panda spends much of its time in trees.
30	A grizzly cub walks along a Rocky Mountain ridge at sunset.

1 2 3 4 5 6 7 8 9 0 Printed in USA 3 2 1 0 9 8 7 6 5 4